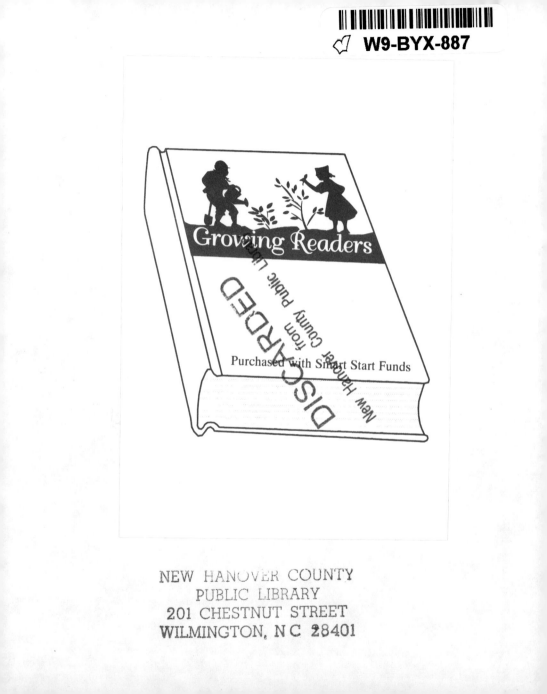

Growing Readers

Purchased with Smart Start Funds

SandCastle 1

What Color is it?

Blue

Mary Elizabeth Salzmann

ABDO
Publishing Company

Published by SandCastle™, an imprint of ABDO Publishing Company, 4940 Viking Drive, Edina, Minnesota 55435.

Printed in the United States.

Cover and Interior Photo credits: Adobe, Diamar, DigitalVision, PhotoDisc

Library of Congress Cataloging-in-Publication Data

Salzmann, Mary Elizabeth, 1968–
    Blue / Mary Elizabeth Salzmann.
        p.   cm. -- (What color is it?)
    Summary: Simple text and pictures introduce things that are blue,
including a pair of overalls, sweater, popsicle, and ball.
    ISBN 1-57765-161-8
    1. Colors--Juvenile literature. 2. Blue--Juvenile literature.
    [1. Blue. 2. Color.] I. Title. II. Series: Salzmann, Mary
Elizabeth, 1968–   What color is it?
    QC495.5.S22   1999
    535.6--dc21
                                                    98-26685
                                                        CIP
                                                        AC

The SandCastle concept, content, and reading method have been reviewed and approved by a national advisory board including literacy specialists, librarians, elementary school teachers, early childhood education professionals, and parents.

Let Us Know

After reading the book, SandCastle would like you to tell us your stories about reading. What is your favorite page? Was there something hard that you needed help with? Share the ups and downs of learning to read. We want to hear from you! To get posted on the Abdo Publishing Company Web site, send us email at:

sandcastle@abdopub.com

About SandCastle™
Nonfiction books for the beginning reader

- Basic concepts of phonics are incorporated with integrated language methods of reading instruction. Most words are short, and phrases, letter sounds, and word sounds are repeated.

- Readability is determined by the number of words in each sentence, the number of characters in each word, and word lists based on curriculum frameworks.

- Full-color photography reinforces word meanings and concepts.

- "Words I Can Read" list at the end of each book teaches basic elements of grammar, helps the reader recognize the words in the text, and builds vocabulary.

- Reading levels are indicated by the number of flags on the castle.

Look for more SandCastle books
in these three reading levels:

| **Level 1**
(one flag) | **Level 2**
(two flags) | **Level 3**
(three flags) |

| **Grades Pre-K to K**
5 or fewer words per page | **Grades K to 1**
5 to 10 words per page | **Grades 1 to 2**
10 to 15 words per page |

My ribbons
are blue.

My sweater is blue.

My ball is blue.

My popsicle is blue.

My overalls
are blue.

My hat is blue.

My inner tube
is blue.

My shirt is blue.

My shirt is blue, too.

Words I Can Read

Nouns

A **noun** is a person, place, or thing

ball (BAWL), p. 9

hat (HAT), p. 15

inner tube (IN-ur TOOB), p. 17

overalls (OH-vur-awlz), p. 13

popsicle (POP-si-kuhl), p. 11

ribbons (RIB-uhnz), p. 5

shirt (SHURT), pp. 19, 21

sweater (SWET-ur), p. 7

Verbs

A verb is an action or being word

are (AR), pp. 5, 13

is (IZ), pp. 7, 9, 11, 15, 17, 19, 21

Sight Words

ball

popsicle

hat

ribbons

inner tube

shirt

overalls

sweater